RADIOACTIVE STARLINGS

PRINCETON SERIES OF CONTEMPORARY POETS

Susan Stewart, *series editor*

For other titles in the Princeton Series of Contemporary Poets see page 85

RADIOACTIVE STARLINGS

Poems

Myronn Hardy

Princeton University Press
Princeton and Oxford

Copyright © 2017 by Princeton University Press

Published by Princeton University Press, 41 William Street,
    Princeton, New Jersey 08540
In the United Kingdom: Princeton University Press, 6 Oxford Street,
    Woodstock, Oxfordshire OX20 1TR

press.princeton.edu

Jacket art: *Mount Sinai*, by Angelbert Metoyer. Courtesy of the artist.

ISBN 978-0-691-17709-0
ISBN (pbk.) 978-0-691-17710-6

Library of Congress Control Number: 2016960849

British Library Cataloging-in-Publication Data is available

This book has been composed in Adobe Garamond Pro

Printed on acid-free paper. ∞

Printed in the United States of America

10 9 8 7 6 5 4 3 2 1

We must unlearn the constellations to see the stars.

—Jack Gilbert

He was the masked fool unmasking the emperor.

—Yusef Komunyakaa

Contents

Pessoa as Starling: New York City 3

Failure 4

Refugees 5

Orpheus Escapes with Turtle 7

Tanner in Tangier: 1912 8

Muddy: A Blues 9

Sea Dark 10

To Mecca with Gold 11

Astronomy Night 12

Devotion 14

Radioactive Starlings 17

Walking Jerusalem 19

Bob Kaufman: 1967 20

Priest with Poinsettia 22

Pork-pie without Sun 23

Pessoa as Starling: Lisbon 25

Existential Guns 26

But I Must Forget 28

The Kneeling: Number 7 30

Faults 32

Hebron 33

Crests 35

Solitary 36

Calling It   39

Two Parallel Shadows of Myronn Hardy   40

Chocolate Liqueur   42

Oud with Guitar: Théâtre National Tunisian   43

Pillars   44

Cobalt   46

Neymar's Hair under Dictatorship   47

Boxed Sandwiches over Algeria   49

The Barber Soloist   50

Pessoa as Starling: Tunis   52

Philosophical Dinner   53

Circles   54

The Inescapable Escape   55

The Breaking   57

Black Typewriter: An Elegy   58

Cascades   59

Ghazal of Wreckage   60

Pessoa as Starling: Johannesburg   62

صباح   63

The Super Looks from the Balcony   64

The Silence in Sunlight   65

At Beethoven's after We Fast   66

Branches   68

Delivering Mint   71

The Ticking   72

Two Bottles of Rain   73

What You Carry   74

The Road Before   75

You: An Apparition   76

Vision near Dumpsters   77

Yellowing   78

Paseo   79

Aubade: Lovely Dark   80

Gwendolyn Brooks Sitting in Tayeb Salih Park Sixteen Years
   after Her Passing   82

NOTES   83

ACKNOWLEDGMENTS   84

PESSOA AS STARLING: NEW YORK CITY

Everything up   climbing up granite   steel.
A poet cries chrysanthemums. A vase
breaks in Harlem on Lenox before meals
are served to nuns   opal beads quick as lace
through conical fingers. A black feather falls
in black hair. His father has black hair sunned
brown in groves where I flew. Poems in groves walled
in loose stones but the poet needed the gun.
The father to send his sighing son to
the city's sighing streets where black women
saunter   sing   carry vases of water
sometimes salty   sometimes fresh. This given
to the poet unconsciously conscious
of riots   the street   the body conscious.

FAILURE

Leaves burn above our heads
yet our hair remains unsinged   black
as jackdaw.

This crispness   this air more
like quince. I have failed miserably.
I have failed you in this

season of colorful death.
How it falls in streets
pounded smooth.

In piles   where I played as a boy.
Auburn joy   now like
the burning of skin.

Who could have known me this way?
This failed man wandering after
the act   after the explosion.

The parachute wide as wilderness   dragging.
This wilderness where
I reach for you.

REFUGEES

Read of refugees wound in acrylic blankets.
Wandering on a hill without walls   walls

to claim   the blast of walls regulatory
in that place   those places returning to loose

mineral   crimson   oyster clouds.
Train stations cloistered but they aren't there.

No acrylic blankets in circles   tubes   stuffed
with the fat of echoes undissolvable despite

the vastness of cerulean.
The graves they have   will

exchange for others.
They are not here. You are told they are not here

but you read this several times   saw the photographs.
Not here.

Not here now.
Wandering   always wandering.

In Amman   a train to Damascus you almost take
but are asked   *Why?* Asked of family.

It is gone   the man who might be
something else says. Something

of pearl   something of dust returned.
Turn from this train.

No dust yet.
Not now.

Sandstone where rivers rubbed red   smooth red.
See this wanderer.

See this.

ORPHEUS ESCAPES WITH TURTLE

Turtle is the audience.
Chords reverberate in the dome   a pattern
of hexagons. How the luthier

stopped breathing after laying
strings   the Alhambra behind him.
But Orpheus doesn't know this

in that shambolic room   neither
the girls who left lace on the floor.
But turtle knows.

Had been there cold on symmetric tiles.
Felt the thump. Knew the cooling would be quick.
Sunbeams as bullets but turtle

kept walking through the shop's opened door.
Sunrise   he thought he'd heard
strumming but it wasn't.

Just a god with a guitar swung to back.
He lifted turtle   took it bagged on the ship.
An apartment on a continent lambent where

turtle is fed sliced apples   spinach on a fissured floor.
Sunrise over hexagons   Orpheus
so obsessed with his making.

TANNER IN TANGIER: 1912

Through a door   there is always light.
My middle name is a door unhinged in Kansas after war.
Starlings follow a dark man wearing white.

He pretends not to see me bite
this pear. Its green   the hue I paint the door.
Through a door   there is always light.

Always God in my hand spilling his might
in oil. Obsessed with the Book   obsessed with lore.
Starlings follow a dark man wearing white.

With what is he obsessed? The light
as shroud   a path to a flat where iron wears hands sore.
Through a door   there is always light.

In the corner   a man sells potatoes gray with blight
near the blue wall   blue as a blues man's core.
Starlings follow a dark man wearing white.

The symmetry of Africa   the *Gateway* in Tangier   African light
like melting malachite. My wife's hand as she dreams of a Moor
through a door. There is always light.
Starlings follow a dark man wearing white.

MUDDY: A BLUES

If I don't go crazy, I will surely lose my mind. –Muddy Waters

Darwish painted on a wall
in Bethlehem. I'm leaning against that wall.
Blue to back   to palms flat as patience.
I lean red coral branches against the wall
yet they won't tentacle about   grace
the poet with sea   to land-lost.
Sea for the poet painted blue on a blue wall.
Blues for the boy who painted
the poet to wall. He listened to Muddy
the night before. His brother's murder
muddy   a muddy street   a muddy
night   red streaks in the mud.

SEA DARK

Graves as the sea waves foam at night.

The graze of shoulder is adulation.

The hand to wrist   its curve the same.

Haunted by satellite   we move to see

more sea   to sit above it   cold.

The folding of it   the folding

of my hand to wrist to hand.

Folding you   me

in a darkness we love.

In a darkness where sea slides

over graves   mosaic.

We are in pieces   ceramic pieces

of color glinting beneath sea.

See how we are?

The sea loving us   waving

over us   cresting over   over.

TO MECCA WITH GOLD

The pale of dark hands warming coins   malleable
coins leaving their remains   the spectacle
of sparkle as silk-laden slaves slip among
sand   slamming against sacks sodden with gold.

Mohamed told me of a grandparent
who sold gold in Mali.
This is recalled in a northern café
when another tells me of Timbuktu   1976

eating salted rice among manuscripts
stained with sun   finger-flicked leaves.
But I'm listening in the cold   in the dark
where waves are loud   echoing through a labyrinth

of salt buildings without a satellite's stout calm.
Tea in Mecca   tea for a king in 1325.
I'm drinking tea in a salt city
as an old man recalls Timbuktu.   Recalls

minarets of earth   a woman
facing Mecca where he stood.

ASTRONOMY NIGHT

You decide to turn   concede the beggar's call.
His hair   branches growing to Khartoum. He believes

you are from Khartoum as you both stand on stones   mossy stones
pressed into earth by Portugal.

This is the consequence of roads   the false conquering of seas.
This meeting   forgotten.

You have been to Khartoum   looked
at your watch as sand swirled fanatically.

A black boy makes a clock in Texas.
His wrists are swallowed by steel.

A bomb   a boy with a bomb his white teacher assumes.
Always assuming destruction.

Always attempting to destroy that which is assumed destroyer.
But who is destroyer?

The destroyed stacked in ground where we walk.
Escape . . .

But there isn't escape.
Perhaps the black of space   staring at black space

from the White House lawn?
A black rocket blasting into black space

from the White House lawn.
You have been to the White House   seen it through black bars.

A black boy leaves Texas   leaves America.
His father says it isn't safe   not for his son.

Never for his son.
A rocket.

Staring at space.
Black space.

Black rocket blasting.
Escape . . .

DEVOTION

But you are quiet because it is gray.
Because chill doesn't pass through coat.
Because the fly   even though flying doesn't pester.
Quiet because it is a kind of creed   the kind
of which you've been viciously devout.
Why give a life to anything else?
Such pain in everything else.
The losing   the loss   thieves
take   leaving you taken.
You've been taken.
What you've done quietly   taken.
History's round   round always gray.

They pretended not to know.

RADIOACTIVE STARLINGS

Starlings on satellite dishes   wait   collect
signals to leave   burst black in air
where ice attempts itself but fails.

White spheres clutter roofs.
White spheres rust on roofs
where starlings rest   leap   signals

in circles sometimes waves meant
to be captured   pulled into wires
displayed on screens   broadcasted

through radios. It is what circulates
through systems   beaks   charged
ochre   florescence through tubes

thinning vibrating bodies almost explosion.
The radioactivity   the gloss of feathers.
No longer just feathers   signals

through the body are invasion.
Invaded starlings on solar panels   granite
crosses peaking steeples   minarets

in constant call: *stop   kneel.*
But starlings take to air   too
many signals to know where.

They collide   break as
if bulbs   clutter
stone streets. Green during

hum   sickly green empties.
This is how we kill   are killing.
Sweepers in uniform drop brooms   ash.

Legs   ash   almost clavicles exposed.
Cars melt   are smelted.
Rising gray funnels   what will fall?

What will fall here?
What has fallen?
Starlings as glass   black   sharp

an abrupt end to the grace
they have given.
Never again   never will

we have this. Starlings as
radioactive gifts in boxes.
Dead starlings in boxes   we

are boxed. Will end in wood
boxes   radioactive
earth will end   will be the end.

WALKING JERUSALEM

Among ashen stone I'm reading "In Jerusalem."
Reading a line   a stanza then walking
about the gray. Shadows lengthen

from feet to wall. Who is kept out?
In a taut twist   some mistake the poem
for cigarette   something else.

But I unravel   read then continue
walking aggrieved. Safety for the almost
destroyed but there is another destruction.

Bread with sesame seeds   I continue to walk.
Gray stones seem larger yet rasped with epochs.
Gabriel with the Prophet ascending near the dome   ascending

to cerulean   a kind of crimson exclusive to sky.
But I'm leaving the poem   sticking it in the wall
where we rock   where we give up plague perpetually present.

Shihab reads the poem in Arabic.
Jerusalem   oh Jerusalem   Darwish
reverberates   "In Jerusalem."

BOB KAUFMAN: 1967

Speak of two seas combining blues. Seeing
those seas   what they are making
me ruminate on this hill. Babble   which
isn't babble as I've chosen not to speak.

Those seas   what they are making
is a line bluer than poetry. This
isn't babble as I've chosen not to speak.
Chosen this as sacrifice. *Sacrifice me in San Francisco*

is a line bluer than poetry. This
rescued from a burning hotel   a portfolio called *Morocco*
charred   chosen as sacrifice. Sacrifice me in San Francisco
while silent   while swimming in a school of sardines.

The golden one   rescued from a burning building
where it acted as marker. I'm acting as poet   hoodoo-holy poet
among the unholy. My face is a crucifixion sight
where a starling grieves in a dying cypress

where it acts as marker. I'm acting as poet   hoodoo-holy poet
not in New Orleans   not in New York but here
where a starling grieves in a dying cypress.
When the war is over   that day   I will burst in a café   recite

not in New Orleans   not in New York but here
in San Francisco. They will listen to me
when the war is over   that day   I will burst in a café   recite
something about ships never sailing. I will speak   break my sacrifice.

In San Francisco they will listen to me.
I will listen to Parker as we listen to Charlie Parker. I will write
something about ships never sailing. I will speak   break my sacrifice
with vibrations   a vibrating throat   blue throat bluer than seas.

PRIEST WITH POINSETTIA

The priest prunes the poinsettia
where a cat climbs   tears the red high in leaves.
The cat climbs higher not wanting to be caught.
The priest's linen robe slogs.
Dead sticks like spears   fall
to travertine   make a kind of sign.
The boys take pictures of the priest
in the tree   lonely length
of red-adorned boughs.
The cat as king tears at the top.
The priest is peculiar in a Muslim country.
How we practice
colonialism   belief   ourselves.
What is our nature?

PORK-PIE WITHOUT SUN

Why wear a pork-pie hat in the park?
So unnecessary as this is low-light   low sun
even though it is morning. A pork-pie hat   tartan

shirt   cotton trousers. He is too conscious
of cirrostratus   all of that in a park   empty.
The only one walking in the park.

The one who climbed from a woman's
window   trousers   pork-pie tight
in hand   no shoes   nothing else on   such

quick feet to filed stone   quick feet
in continuously cursed air. Curses
through the window from the man with

whom she lived but he was supposed
to be away. That is what he told her.
He was going south to see his mother.

She cried   something about missing   unendurable
but pork-pie found her. Her room found him
after cold oak benches   convening

on cold oak benches in the empty
park   eucalyptus swaying.
But he is alone.

Still wearing his pork-pie but has
never eaten pork. Nothing religious   just
a decision about blood   no blood in his mouth.

He is resting on the bench   pork-pie covers face.
A woman   the same woman watches   hears
him sleep   places a sheaf of wheat   seven

marigolds   their stems long over him.
She leaves the park   leaves herself between
the park   the waft of blistering bread.

PESSOA AS STARLING: LISBON

My father is dead as is my brother.
Absence is invisibility but
I feel   feel them in currents folding through
feathers   hills where cathedrals collide with
unconsciousness. Starshine glares with such whiteness
like crests. I dive into the hard crests of
this land like the Atlantic   salty with
subjugation. Not a bird of prey but
preyed upon. My silence   so insincere.
I tell you of this place   transcribe it through
another name   a man I make up   sing
to perhaps in a dream   through possession.
Call me mysterious. Alone   without
flock   I claim no one but they will claim me.

EXISTENTIAL GUNS

We sit.
We eat.
We hold
cats in
laps. We
think while
choosing vegetables:
Why is
broccoli itself?
The moon
    we stare
unlike wolves
that howl.
Time sometimes
drips   pours.
We kill
that which
keeps us.
Guns in
piles. We
are grasping
guns. We
feel the
searing. We
want it
set. Set
it up.
Set it
off. We
are set
to do

it. Have
done it.
Keep doing
it despite
the sear
    the mark
of Mars
    how maverick
this manipulation.

BUT I MUST FORGET

I must travel to a paradise of ashes,
walk among its hidden trees.–Adonis

Sit for bread   honey   a glass of tea.
The dead rest in piles.
Damascus is the dust you carry cautiously.
Clothes cumbersome with dust but
this is how it remains   you remain of its dust.
Define weary.
Worry about the unburied   their silver
cords snapped. They ascend to smoking
towers but still gaze the piles
of themselves   the cinders of civilization.
To be civil means to be at peace.
But peace is processed through its opposite.
This is what you understand   what you've
heard   what you impatiently expect.
Lost here   lost but must forget.
What did Dylann Roof forget?
Entering the church as some form
of dead to make others dead   to kill
them among a grace he couldn't enter.
It couldn't enter him   so fallen   such
gracelessness the unburied see
where he will fall   the tunnel
that will pull   the tunnel
with teeth tunneling tighter.
The church   three times
destroyed by tribe   nature.
Roof's innovation
with gun   youth.
Taken by police with civility.

Not dragged   shot
in the back   shoulder   side.
Steel rings gently circled   escorted
to car. Trying to
love. That church   you never
loved   those people dead.
Did you love them   all those
like them dead in churches?
Dead in Damascus?

THE KNEELING: NUMBER 7

Cottonwood leaves helix to ground.
Gold on ground in the shape of clubs
but this club is a country. A song
of a country played in stadiums

but outside steel veins   danger.
History's danger   the present
we are given perpetually.
Accept in boxes we unribbon.

But some of us kneel on green blades
despite the stains they leave.
Despite the quiet sound of desiccating leaves.
Their falling.

Their whirling
to blades   the helixes
of wide hair in which they lodge.
Hair picked into space   no rim seen.

We play in space without the object of play.
But we catch   throw as if it were.
Black space in Mexico City where we
return to play with black gloves clinched.

So much running   we ran then stood silently.
Starlings   we heard   imagined hearing.
A song unlike the one making us kneel.
Clatter of steel   we kneel.

Kneel here knowing the clatter.
Knowing this club of clatter.
You armed me with strength for battle
but this battle

has broken the battle.
Gold falls here.

FAULTS

A star cracks the mud on your face.
An earth veined with faults.
Your fault you are floating

in a sea so salty it is dead.
The leaves of holy books
float as if bread.

Starlings will not come to feast
even though you believe they
will   bread almost liquid.

It is like the bread you had with lunch.
The bread you tore before dipping in hummus.
How the holy land looms.

Rufous mountains are folded
in fog a star can't crack.
Whose fault is this?

HEBRON

Green awnings have rusted.
Time unstill   you are unstill
walking on a street stilled.

Your mind holds the no longer market.
You want to show me the market.
You have crawled prison floors.

Your son has done the same.
You are the same   the ceaselessness.
Your mother served green olives after you

were released but what is release?
You see barbed wire.
Are cut by it in sleep.

Ghosts slide from slits.
Soldiers in green uniforms walk
about the city   patrol it before

eating green olives at home.
They ask for your papers.
There is danger in their asking   in their

surrounding   their makeshift grove   in being yourself.
At home   you offer me the hearts
of lettuce   a different green   tender green.

In the past   we rested
among saddled horses. Buildings
were faint   sand saturated air.

We will not leave   will not enter sea   sink.
Seaweed as sea groves   the sea
will not hold this green.

CRESTS

Crests the color of houses
walled in fog. She can't see

the houses as crests dissolve in blue.
Miles Davis dissolves in a room

with white tiles where she walks
without wondering why.

That soft pacing as a woman leaves
a house because she chooses lucidity.

Chooses it as crests fall to feet   salt
over feet that burns. It matters that they

burn on a beach she'd only seen   never
walked with urgency or reluctance.

Those houses   where are they?
Sightlessness the color of crests   the color

of fog   the color of teeth in sea
creatures clamoring clandestinely.

She remembers a song   a shiny
trumpet rendering spring but it's

not spring even though jasmine
blooms in crest-colored cups.

SOLITARY

The sea desires to dissolve stone.
Turn the serrated into itself   into a kind
of somber   into white bubbles   into blue.
Surprised by this solitary view of cliff.
Calcium edifices mimic afterlife.
What does air ask in its violence?
The sea more violent   my hands
contorting over stone but I let them free.
The back of my head   an opened
slot releasing a vermilion ribbon.
Waves in the waves   the arcs tangle
deeper   summon sharks. A gift
to the cold   a sacrifice to moonlight   to
the dark   to my unhealable wound.

CALLING IT

Among the wandering   the mist-drenched street
where snail soup is slurped   cinnamon
as ghost in the mouth   you here.
Shimmering dust   shimmering silver   something
galactic seen through telescope but here   plain sight
an occasion for Roman candles   bottle
rockets   sparklers surrounding cake.
But none of that   just the sphere made
by extremities. The reaching around void no
longer void but wool   goose feathers   skin.
The reign of silence   the dates eaten
only at night suddenly over   suddenly
orange blossom water   ginger on fingers.
Sit   stare   let me do it. Let me
outline   shadow the being you've become.
The migrant I've sought   seen near
sea   my pacing near sea each morning
where seagulls   starlings watch   see
inside me hibiscus vines growing in crude.
Their happiness   complacency
challenged by sight   seeing me   sea
wanderer sullied among sunbeams.
But no more   you are here.
Tomorrow we will walk along
sea cresting our feet. Seagulls   starlings
will see something else   call
something else sea.

TWO PARALLEL SHADOWS OF MYRONN HARDY

One more waxen than the other   a tunnel

to a gravel vein made visible by streetlights

or the moon   colossal   copper

above the cedars.

The weight of heather in weightless air.

The rabid Rottweiler tied to a stump   barking

at a burning pile of garbage   at the shadows

lengthening on the tarred street.

He hates shadows   their ability

to shift   to cast over   take away light.

But two shadows of one man: the seen life   the life

made on paper   synapses as lightning in a violet sky.

These two speak to each other as the dog loses

its bark   as heather mingles with catalpa.

The shadows see Pegasus   trace the constellation

with fingers   no flight   no wings   shadows

long on black streets.

Starlings asleep in catalpa branches.

They see the shadows in dream.

Have known the shadows without meeting.

Have seen their maker without

shadows near sea   near mountain.

Have followed him not seeing his shadows

or the ones they made about him.

Meet us here   near streetlights   on tarred

streets   near cedars   the two of us imperiled.

CHOCOLATE LIQUEUR

Speak of the misfortunate confiscation.
The look of your hands without
the bottle   their hands with it
wondering what's inside.
The digestif they'd taste after dinner.
I surprise with a flask dripping
chocolate liqueur into our coffee.
The rum factory where we watched
the burning blue of it curl in cream cups.
Never coffee like this   a show of blue
in brown   froth at the lip.
We ponder dusk   the honey locusts
almost leafless   Havana last May.
The you   you are   now cultivated
through years in a peculiar
field gone green. Somewhere else
the cultivation   the same
green   the hands as brown as
the fields where they fell.
The tall green that took   buried   drank
them into green.
More chocolate   more liqueur in our cups.
The you   you are greening.

OUD WITH GUITAR:
THÉÂTRE NATIONAL TUNISIAN

He leans against the glass door.
In the back   he listens to musicians
pluck the audience to trance.
He bought an oud in Istanbul   practiced
in Fez then gave up   a life quickly
convoluted. His fingers bleed.
But he listens to oud with guitar in the dim
room where we sip coffee. When he
looks at the closed stage door   he sees
starlings leaving through the roof   darkening sky with dots.
Oud with guitar   a kind of crash.
We are a kind of crash.
We forget   never realize
this   marching in cadence.

PILLARS

These pillars   how they have stood
unlike poplars never guarding
anything but used to hoist the once

alive   recently mutilated   their
weighty sway.
On steps among shaped marble aiming

at ice attempting itself   you notice
the lilac. It is spring.
A girl licking something sweet   round   that

which dissolves to missiles.
Who plays the song climbing through the window?
The song suddenly breeze swirling

about that flapping flock.
Black iridescence in blue   a
malformed tunnel   true.

Black bestowed   speckled   gold
beaks breaking blue.
You

do
sit among pillars   cold.
But they have always been cold

unlike you.
There among them   exposed   tampered   made
into themselves by empire   like you.

That piano   that woman's voice
flocking about you   about the flock
forming itself.

COBALT

There is cobalt in the voice.
In the saunter beneath the budding oak
where moss festers on the dark trunk.
How cobalt satellites ears   warms
capillaries   curls the mouth.

We don't have to say it.
No redundancy to wreck rotating wheels.
We turn   turn in ourselves to know
whom we are becoming   the grace
of which we are being wrought.

NEYMAR'S HAIR UNDER DICTATORSHIP

When a banana is thrown in the stadium   your
teammate takes   peels   eats yet you
don't see its implication   the hook's inclusion of you.
Its violation of your existence   our existence?

This is curious.
How the Americas invest in imagination
meant to annihilate you   us. That truth
opulent in your barber's chair.

Nuclear war–waged hair.
Decimated curl   scalp of pale-dead corpses you love.
What controls you?
Manipulates that which is so close to brain?

The crucifix of history   a blond beam over black water.
You are so young.
See the self.
Sift the self.

See
Not the body moving over field but it   the internal.
See it fully.
See us.

See?
See it without that mighty madness
crusted on since arrival   before. Not your fault   now.
But it will be if you don't see.

See?
When you see   raise your arms
with knees to green ground.
Hear us   hear you cheer.

BOXED SANDWICHES OVER ALGERIA

Mourn the destination. Its jaggedness
displayed in mountains meant to cut if crash.
The jacaranda-lined avenues   forget how they
hacked branches   purple blossoms to tar.

Something beautiful is dead.
Something beautiful should not have died.
No resuscitation in that city   move
to another reluctantly.

Sandwiches of carrots   red
Cabbage   mustard   revolutionary
sandwiches   vegetables are revolutionary
because there is no blood. Nothing running

away from something sharp shimmering sun.
We are whimsical.
We are revolutionaries watching
flamingos flock south.

THE BARBER SOLOIST

Not two people   not two gifts   clippers
vibrate in strands until they fall
gracefully to the floor   like petals
concert stagehands sweep   wonder

from where they were plucked.
I'm onstage after blades
have straightened lines   sideburns
edged to squares   alcohol burning.

Cotton scarf tied about neck.
Its mauve stripes chameleon strings
strummed with a powdered bow.
I'm not a boy.

This is not a school concert where
parents clap for their nervous child.
I'm a man nervous
in my shop paid for with loans.

The bank owns everything.
I see myself in mirrors
where I'm habitually invisible.
My lids forced over pupils.

I can't   won't see me.
I'm solo.
This is a solo.
They are listening.

The four here are listening   strings
quiver like clippers   like ficus
branches   like palm fronds
when wind whips.

I have practiced like wind.
Practiced in an apartment
shared with two Dobermans
I feed fleshly bones.

They have listened without
howl   with ears erect   spines
as if pulled tall with tide.
Practiced at night   practiced

on balconies overlooking desolation.
Don't desert me now.
Not after   during the solo   my
solo solving me.

PESSOA AS STARLING: TUNIS

That hollow building built in 1923
is a cage with windows
wide as wild. I fly over
Avenue Habib Bourguiba   perch
in trees pruned to green squares wondering
when again   the raucousness   the fragility
belief anchors.
My song is silence but theirs is not.
The rhythm of subversion
after nothing   after everything
red dries to skin. Tanks ready
to blast   barbed wire in pythons   military
on guard all warning to never
rage   never ask   never human   never.

PHILOSOPHICAL DINNER

We were offered fish   glasses of wine.
A framed photograph of Albert Camus
rested on top of books made to tower.
There is a mistake   mine as I

believed   briefly the photo was
that of Mehdi Ben Barka. His
apartment in Paris among towers
dusty with premonition.

We are meaningful because
we've decided to be.
If Ben Barka had spoken in Havana   how
would we be here? We with glasses

of wine as riots rouse
towns fermenting to vinegar.
The ongoing hollowing of ourselves   we
are the assassins of ourselves.

CIRCLES

Time as whirlpool   the ousting of despots.
How flags flap on string wound to light poles.
Red flags with white circles   red hooks
thrown to stars unhooked.
She bathes in sun over the avenue.
Her hands spin   an ushering.
She doesn't see the boy on that same
avenue selling paper geraniums in plastic tubes.
The shadow of the clock on his back   the numbers
subtracting   red   oh red.

THE INESCAPABLE ESCAPE

The stairs behind him lead to a room always locked.
Three old women sitting in plastic chairs speak
without being heard by the boy looking beyond

the house   at men drinking tea   arguing
for a life mere theory.
Pine   almond tree branches

weighted with nuts.
He eats almonds seeing white blossoms
in fields never walked.

Walk with me here.
Beyond the corroded gate   after its corroded sound
scatters finches   itself through streets.

Escape with me as did my family   some
of them frozen in this ground.
We will not freeze.

It is spring   mint in the ground   mint
in tea   rose in tea   we will drink tea.
It will boil beneath minerals   skin.

Let's play on wet ground until
our shoes are mud.
We are clay   water   forever returning.

The stairs behind the women lead to a room always locked.
They are standing near the gate   listening for the boy
who yells   such joy in that voice.

The innocence they had to lose to live.
Pieces of ourselves off   up   the wind takes.
We let it.

We are taken   learn
to forgive this thievery
but never wanting to see it.

Know that kind
of defeat   that horrific clarity.
The women begin to sing.

THE BREAKING

There is disaster.
The kind that climbs boughs
to find blue breaking about itself.

Breaking because it must   so
high   such neglect there as we
are unwilling to attempt such glory.

The vastness of it   the struggle
against gravity.
Disaster laughs at itself as what

it had planned already ensues.
The translucence
of it   its expansion.

We breathe it.
We drink it.
We are . . .

BLACK TYPEWRITER: AN ELEGY

Type while wearing a T-shirt   a typewriter

with blue keys on the T-shirt. A black

T-shirt worn by a black poet.

It is Christmas Eve. Two black

boys play matador   bull

on Avenue Ibn Rochd. They parody

excitable spectators   red cloth

as trickster   such safety in wool peacoats.

Their father kneels to tie

his son's slack shoestrings.

Trayvon Martin's remain untied.

His father continues to kneel.

CASCADES

Leave me as there is no integrity.
Nothing in the cascades
foaming against volcanic rock.
Nothing in the magma of hands   crimson

pools beneath spiraling layers.
Nothing yet there is pulse.
The rhythm of which we wandered
the dark   the avenues black with still.

Leave me without music.
The music made without speaking   without tuba.
Nothing but smoke   melted ice in glasses.
Nothing but wind near the river   pirates

watching from the other side.

GHAZAL OF WRECKAGE

The intent was safety   affable confinement beneath the black
of sky but there was boom. Steel seams releasing the black

in blue. Tumultuousness in funnels never meant for sky's
eye   rings in the blue. This wreckage   this release of the black

mined maliciously. Greed as God   the almighty deity   the lie
inexplicably true. The captain is dead seeing the black

from black sky. Seeing swirling spheres   waves. *I'm
the cause. Blame me.* The captain has wrecked the black.

He has wrecked me yet I still float   in pieces   have failed
in pieces   know corrosion in pieces   pieces never intact. The black

is innocent yet made to surround anemones   sink
silver schools   saturate sand sticky. The black

sky can do nothing for its black brother   a xylophone
of color without percussive potential. What we do to the black

is take   everything taken as it takes the blue.
As I sluggishly sink in the black

growing   separating into crude starlings.
They are lifting into wind   wings viscous. The black

of them drips into the blue they have left   been made.
Circles   circles   metaphysical gyre in the black

sky as they call   as they know the turning   a
phase   a period turning the black

dripping into its remains. Most of the moon
is black. A sliver opposes the black

it is. The sea is. The oil birds are. Ezra isn't asleep.
But pacing   feeling his wreckage wounding the black.

PESSOA AS STARLING: JOHANNESBURG

Dark feathers stuffing the pillow.
The feathers of my dead brother   you
sleep there on his feathers sewed in muslin.
You were born when Brazil ended slavery.
When my great-grandfather watched a black
woman sob beneath a pale awning.
Mahatma Gandhi hated blacks   arrived
in Durban when your father died. You knew
this disabling place even though young.
Sleeping on black feathers   black
illusions during sleep   such serenity.
We are pitch in a chromatic sky shrinking.
I was the bird who sang to another.

صباح

Meet me beneath the brocaded awning
where light cuts the iron table.
Where I'm leaning in a bamboo chair
pondering an arch's age   how green
shoots jut from stone. The police in black
uniforms prance the cobbled center dangling rifles.
A city slow on Sunday   wanted to see it open.
Left you in the room sleeping on pale
sheets   pillows   pears on the nightstand.
Wanted to sit.
Wanted to let you wake without me to feel stillness.
Wanted you to open curtains needing
to find me   needing to walk   needing
the quiver of maybe. But you
know nearing the arch   nearing
the awning as police stare ready
to cock cold guns   arms unspool.

THE SUPER LOOKS FROM THE BALCONY

The silence   the cerulean   a sea of cerulean
as they slip on shoes. They are leaving
the new mosque   walking down marble
stairs to the sidewalk where two young men

hold round loaves like books.
Bread after prayer another kind of food.
They are selling bread because one assumes
prayer makes men hungry. They are hungry   their

reason for selling steaming loaves in bags.
A caped man watches from the balcony.
The pale building with blue doors   windows
shaped like giant tuna   caped man is the super.

His black cape covers hands.
He wants to fly down   buy   divide
loaves for those who prayed   speckled
birds that always pray.

That super isn't super but he wants to be.
If he could fly down   he'd be super.
The young men would give him a loaf.
It would certainly glow.

They would glow.
The cape would glow.
We would wash   pray
again   buy glowing loaves.

THE SILENCE IN SUNLIGHT

after Ieshia Evans

The rigorousness of silence made her silent.

Made air grace her sundress silently

strung to back in the morning.

Her back not poplar   magnolia

yet it is brown.

Met by men armored in black.

Silence as armor   her armor after numbness.

Black gun to black body in black cotton.

Silence within the silence within the air.

AT BEETHOVEN'S AFTER WE FAST

The cannon's blast means we can begin with water.
Begin again   the earth again flooded   renewed.
Soup of vegetables   beans   we sit on a deck

that has lost its stain   its protection.
The sky protects us   azure turning onyx.
We are silent in our rejuvenation.

Honey locust boughs sway as starlings fall
to feed on the bread a woman tears
because she is torn from herself.

Her life   someone else's
but that realization is the tearing   the bread
she tears   that motion   compression

of hands   fingers   her silence among that fervent flock.
But we are replenishing that which
we relinquished voluntarily.

Drops on our fingers   transparent   cold.
Not the forecast we read that morning delirious
with the knowledge of the desert we'd walk   tomes

in camel-skin bags we'd discuss in a room with drawn blinds.
But the drops become solid   bounce on the deck   the ground.
We stand beneath an awning saddened

by the beauty of ice. Beauty that could
pummel   bouncing   breaking.
Who breaks?

Who understands the broken?
Who collects   continues to collect
everything we claim we are not?

BRANCHES

Find ficus branches scattered on slate.
A waiter slips   slams against
the café window but doesn't fall.

He is surprised   perturbed looking
at ladders   tall where cutters
descend holding their blades.

There is sorrow in that display
of fallen green. The cutters   from the slick
street load branches into the trunk.

Their brown uniforms keep us aware
of the ground where we will fall.
Where we will give up the world.

DELIVERING MINT

To wake before the sun's belligerent beams.
To receive pale wood crates.
To see beneath dissolving Cepheus.
To his dry hand against damp stems.
To a kind of effervescence.
To the bursting of morning.
To tying stems to bunch other stems.
To toss in the wheelbarrow.
To wheel on pavement.
To watch bees buzz over herbaceousness.
To stop in cafés with green bouquets to green glasses.
To give themselves up there.
To grieve the death of green.
To see his shirt inexplicably green.

THE TICKING

A parked van in the shadow of an olive tree
where leaves hang over the wall in knives.

My lover sees the van as a missile buzzing   unlaunched.
A bomb   really   a clock inside: tick   tick.

She kisses me hearing pulse   everything
pulse. A twelve-year-old boy   a cop's bullet

breaks in the boy   we on the verge of pop.
Beggars by the van recall the bombs behind them.

The fired holes in forests   the surviving starlings
circling flame   the dying or meant to die.

There will be more.
We know this.

Blocks of blue cheese   brie
from the basket   my lover slices

on butcher block   tomatoes   bulbs of fennel.
She rubs her hand through rosemary

hedges   through my hair: tick   tick.
What is inside the skull?

Explosion?
The ending of explosion?

We are in grass.
Lying in grass.

TWO BOTTLES OF RAIN

In a wood known for lakes   two bottles
of rain are collected during a storm.

Your eyes as lakes drying to earth ocher   the stones
about your neck. Those bottles on asphalt white

with the arid sex of poplars.
The desolation of night   that feeling of alone

then tranquillity then the choice not to see.
You not passing quiet bottles

of clatter   wet clatter of storm.
My grandmother washes her hair in rainwater.

She is blind in one eye yet sees me not seeing
you   this love of darkness countering the world.

WHAT YOU CARRY

Buy string beans   pumpkin   pimentos.
They are heavy against the back. That weight
usually against the chest   usually

at night   the dream of the body.
Its breathing syncopated in dream   syncopated
at night   there at night but not there.

Absence as force   spheres of volcanic rock
against the chest where the body should be.
Question weight   question oak

beams   the ceiling's strength   your
strength as you carry vegetables   as you
see the body awake   the body laughing

outside the market. Laughing at a joke told
by another body. Another body unaware
of you   the era of you when starlings

gathered in pines. Where you
pointed   *even the birds*   you said.
But now they aren't here.

Look at me
as I look away   as
I love away you.

THE ROAD BEFORE

Before the road was paved
it was dust   bits of gravel.
We were love   then surrounded

in its rust billow squinting to keep
its grit from tearing our eyes.
How it rose as if dahlias from

grassy earth   fell with
winter   quickly crippled.
How I hate walking on this now

rock road   nothing surrounding
me   nothing rust.
The single starling in the sycamore

looks green. A witness to
the tarring   its toxic smoke that
billowed   subsumed the nest

the bird wouldn't leave
rendering the tree sickly.
Oh love   the mourning   this green

morning when I walk
without sound. Where I walk
startled by a green bird.

YOU: AN APPARITION

The you not there.
The you I think of beneath yellow leaves.
The you I love beneath yellow leaves.
The sun's yellow rendering me
without courage to appear where
you are   the apparition
I am where you sleep.
I'm the intensity in the room.
Your hands over eyes can't save sight.
Let the yellow blister
as you have blistered me.
Oh love   look.
On the nightstand   the clay bowl of lemons.
One is molding blue.
We dive there   spores
make us cough.
How damp this blue
with you not even there.

VISIONS NEAR DUMPSTERS

The dark is vision.
I'm visionary with a burning
cigarette among dumpsters.

I lean   find fried potatoes   fish
heads that stare back afraid of me   afraid
of the dark without water.

The boys in black jackets are shadow
against blue buildings.
Why do I hear "Blue in Green" in the dark?

Why now as I smoke?
My father walking through Tangier
with a bouquet of lilies.

This is the last. Petals are buildings
fading into each other   the paper
around the cigarette before the burn.

The smolder is the moon   then nothing.
Nothing said to the visionary near dumpsters.
The boys in black jackets see   know

nothing but I see them   me   them
through smoke.
My father   oh my father   I see.

YELLOWING

What becomes of a man in love with cardamom?
Who sits in a café in Amman staring at a city soused
in smoke smelling of apple orchards?
How he ate apples in fall.
The tree in his parents' yard dropped yellowing fruit
when juice went wine.
He doesn't drink wine.
But apple smoke plumes from a nose narrow yet tall.
Tell me of homelands lost.
Tell me of palms tall with yellowing leaves.
Tell me of wandering as yellow taxis
shadow a yellow sun sinking.
Canaries leaving yellowing ruins
singing a yellow song.

PASEO

Pomegranate blossoms on paper   she
is drawing pomegranate blossoms on paper
while wearing pomegranate blossoms in dark hair.

A red explosion in a fallow field   no
harvest. The Atlantic is loud as we
pass   hold its blue in our slowing brains.

Cones of sunflower seeds   we pour
in palms   pop in mouth. If they land on ground
no fields   no reminders of sun   nothing tall

swaying   nothing hypnotic.
In a background of crashing   we are walking slowly.
Stars as streetlights   the streets are dirty.

They are scrubbing the floors of the fish market
as there are no more fish.
Everything sold.

Suds on marble like the crests you see.
No starlings on ruined balconies   in date palms drying.
No news of murders   those drowned.

The floating we can't see   such tumult.
A playwright is buried in the Christian cemetery.
He faces the sea perpetually.

She pulls pomegranate blossoms
from her hair   leaves them on the pale grave.
Her hair   now in waves   wind in the waves.

AUBADE: LOVELY DARK

Absence   how it begins to trickle
in that sealed place. The sacred

opening of blinds like peonies
or four-o'clocks without redolence.

The moon is gone.
The mother-of-pearl buttons   circles

on your coat flung on that hard chair.
What will it say when you sit?

Drape its cotton   its silk
lining over naked shoulders?

The absence like rainwater   cold.
Drink this cold water.

Wash your hair with cold rainwater.
We are running.

Stop beneath the awning where your hair
swirls about my fingers in curled ribbons.

The ribbons you tied about your waist.
They coiled then fell then coiled.

They were the color of peonies
or four-o'clocks.

I'm leaving before the sky is white.
Before absence loops my feet to carpet.

Before the brass knob ceases to turn.
Oh love   the turning.

Why must we turn this
lovely dark to day?

GWENDOLYN BROOKS SITTING IN TAYEB SALIH PARK SIXTEEN YEARS AFTER HER PASSING

We occur. Are occurring among hibiscus   hibiscus tea in the morning
without sugar   white plates of hibiscus in the park. Have their mothers
been to Mecca   walked around the box? This oak bench is a box within
a clover box recently trimmed. This is the north but I call it south   not the South
Side but the south. South of Chicago   the oldest south we will never recall.
I recall the prize. The lights didn't work. Then they did. The house flickered.
We occur. Are occurring here. A poet is writing on a balcony. We met in Chicago
where he gave me two poems he'd published in a journal. I wrote to him.
He is writing on a balcony obsessed with waves. I'm waving to waves   the large
ship spewing smog. Starlings peck in clover. I wave to them. Their wings
are waving. Black wings wave over blue waves breaking. All of this
breaking   who is broken? Boys in school uniforms but their shoes are free.
Neon free. Like neon signs in the dark   see me. In this park   they leap.
Look at the waterless fountain   hear the sea. They see me   the south
in me   think   *we occur everywhere*. Think   think   have known migrants.
Have known themselves as migrants but not now.
They are settled   leaping.

Notes

"Astronomy Night": On September 14, 2016, Ahmed Mohamed, a fourteen-year-old Muslim student at MacArthur High School in Irving, Texas, was accused, by a teacher, of having brought a bomb into the school. It was actually a clock he had made. He was arrested and escorted out of the school building handcuffed. President Barak Obama invited him to participate in an astronomy night at the White House.

"But I Must Forget": Dylann Roof, a white supremacist, killed nine people while they were worshipping at the Emanuel African Methodist Episcopal Church in Charleston, South Carolina, June 17, 2015.

"The Silence in Sunlight": Photograph taken by Jonathan Bachman, July 9, 2016, of Ieshia Evans protesting the shooting of Alton Sterling in Baton Rouge, Louisiana.

"Philosophical Dinner": Mehdi Ben Barka (1920–65) was a Moroccan politician and revolutionary. He disappeared in Paris, October 1965.

Acknowledgments

Grateful acknowledgment goes to the editors of the following journals, in which some of these poems first appeared: *Borderlands: Texas Poetry Review*, *Hungry Mountain*, *Miracle Monocle*, *Versal*, *Seneca Review*, *Interim*, and *Poet Lore*.

"Tear It Down" is from *Collected Poems* by Jack Gilbert, copyright © 2012 by Jack Gilbert. Used by permission of Alfred A. Knopf, an imprint of the Knopf Doubleday Publishing Group, a division of Penguin Random House LLC. All rights reserved.

Excerpt from "Omens" from *The Emperor of Water Clocks* by Yusef Komunyakaa. Copyright ©2015 by Yusef Komunyakaa. Reprinted by permission of Farrar, Straus and Giroux.

"Mean Red Spider," by McKinley Morganfield, copyright © 1948 by Warner/Chappell Music, Inc, BMG Rights Management US, LLC (sung by Muddy Waters).

"Flower of Alchemy" from *Selected Poems* by Adonis. Translated by Khaled Mattawa, Yale University Press, 2010, p. 59.